Other creations by
Stewart S. Warren

HeartLink.com

WAY OF THE CURRENT

TAROT
REFLECTIONS

Stewart S. Warren

Way of the Current
Tarot Reflections

ISBN: 978-1-940769-20-2
Publisher: Mercury HeartLink
Printed in the United States of America

Tarot card images:
Tarot de Marseille, Jean Dodal 1701
Restitution by Jean-Claude Flornoy,
courtesy Roxanne Flornoy

Contact: *editor@heartlink.com*

Mercury HeartLink
www.heartlink.com

Introduction

Tree of Life Illustrations

Suit of *Wands*
Spots: Ace through Ten
Royals: Knave, Knight, Queen, King

Suit of Cups
Spots: Ace through Ten
Royals: Knave, Knight, Queen, King

Suit of Swords
Spots: Ace through Ten
Royals: Knave, Knight, Queen, King

Suit of Coins
Spots: Ace through Ten
Royals: Knave, Knight, Queen, King

High Cards
Fool through World, Fool again

WAY OF THE CURRENT

INTRODUCTION

When working with the Tarots, either in divination or personal contemplation, the "spots" (so named for arrangement of suit elements on numbered cards in non-pictorial decks) are often associated with events and conditions in time and space—the stuff happening in our day to day doing. These conditions and events are by no means shallow and random and can be identified by the emanationist in relation to their positions on the Qabalistic Tree of Life. It is from that system that I have drawn some, though not all, of my inspiration when working with the numbered cards. But this isn't anything new. It's evident to me that Ms. Smith and Dr. Waite [Ryder-Waite-Smith Tarot] also used the Qabalah, along with their complex system of astrological correspondences, to arrive at a symbolism that has greatly influenced western esotericism through that famous deck published in 1910. Some of my understanding has come through those more recent and intermediary schools of thought, nevertheless, we will now leave that branch and brand of occultism and see how those ancient systems work in this book.

I personally enjoy working with *Tarot de Marseille* style decks because they are void of picture "narratives" on the spots allowing a wider range of possibilities. When we're working in the realm of intuition and subtle energies I think it important to consider this. With the Spots—Aces through Tens—I have worked largely with Pythagorean Number Theory, the Elements, and the Tree of Life, but not exclusively. Following this introduction are two graphic representations of the Tree of Life, one envisioned by Rabbi Isaac Luria, "the Ari", which demonstrates the so-called "fall of man," or the divorce of humankind from both heaven and the feminine, and another more balanced tree that I modified from the earlier Natural Array as dictated by the Gra version of the Tree. I assigned only the numbers, respecting your own understanding and system of coordinates.

In brief, the 10 Sephirot of the Qabalah have, over time, come to represent successive stages of emanation from the One down through increasingly more complex stations of organization to finally arrive at the Ten—in four "worlds." We call this Creation. There is an intelligent journey going on here, both descending (involving) and ascending (evolving), depending on whether you are traveling "down" or "up" the Tree. There are ten Sephira in four worlds; there are ten numbered cards in four suits—et viola! The Internet and good brick and mortar bookstores have a myriad of resources on this subject. Please avail yourself of the work of true scholars and mystics.

When it comes to the Royals, or court cards, my approach has been to draw upon both western spiritualism and psychology. You will no doubt notice the associations with Jungian "types." One—and only one—of the approaches to the Royals is to consider them in terms of their age, which leads to an understanding of stages of maturity or personal development. Here we can see the wide-eyed sophomoric innocence of the Knave, the energetic resolve of the Knight, the established interior power of the Queen, and the outwardly engaging mastery of the King. And based on that, each one has their shadow, or misaligned and undeveloped aspect. Each of us possess all sixteen modes, as we continually engage the various and repeating stages of development in own our lives.

The royal family (our own interior constellation) is also understood here to reference gender in the following way. Gender is about the generation, or re-generation, of life. At any given moment we may be receptive or active in relationship to the energies of the Divine Impulse that we receive and express. *Actually, it's all happening simultaneously.* So the Queen of Wands within you will have a different view and function than that of the King of Wands, one court member being more inner defined, the other more outer oriented. Each of these "players" is an archetype, but also a message bearer from Source. Here we consider maturity, element, gender and link to higher realms. No good guys, no bad guys, just souls experiencing life on earth using the dynamic aspects of personality.

The High Cards, or Major Arcana, are the most discussed in other Tarot books, but I'm going to keep it very simple. Of all the many, many ways that this compendium of perennial wisdom can be approached, I think of the High Cards in terms of powers, patterns and indications of process. For me, they represent stages of emanation, and therefore *stages of spiritual evolution*, from the tiniest form of life to the most expansive and grand, from densest matter to the highest vibrations beyond which we can imagine. At the same time, they represent *states of consciousness*. To say more would be less— I defer to the wisdom of your own gnosis.

To briefly recap some possible functions of the Tarot in divination—our conversation with God—I'll hit the highlights again. The forty Spots show us, within a system that dynamically reflects the stages of creation itself, where we are in terms of a specific situation, a condition or lesson, that we have paused in divination in order to better understand. The Royals provide further information about how our personality, an entity also in divine flux, is responding to, or might respond to, internal and external stimuli, and our degree of spiritual maturity with that. The High Cards tell us what cosmic and karmic forces, beyond space and time, are actively in the foreground of the issues at hand, and something about the greater needs of our individual and collective soul that are influencing this moment. As "mirror of the soul," the Tarot is a link between our conscious and subconscious mind, accurately reflecting the All as we learn how to frame our questions to life, and how to listen to her reply.

This little book of images and commentary is not an introduction to Tarot, nor is it an in-depth exploration. *Way of the Current,* however, is an invitation. Those who know all about western esotericism and the Tarot tradition will find it incomplete and even contradictory, however...

those who have a *beginners mind* will find fresh perspectives and inspiration for further reflection. My intention is to provide additional starting points for your personal inquiry. As well, I hope to suggest a continuity within, and also across, the three components of the Tarot, and to create curiosity about things like *why* the 7 seeks the balance of the 8. And perhaps, together, we'll develop more of a "felt sense" for the holistic nature of this ancient and evolving tool for transformation.

Phrases like "cube of space" will hopefully stand poetically on their own, but for the mystic they might prompt more investigation. Not only do I trust your ability to set up your own methods of learning, I believe absolutely in the inherent ability of your subconscious to integrate, synthesize and deliver dynamic and pertinent meaning. If your rational mind stumbles over sentence fragments or archaic syntax, just say to yourself, "I am reading poetry."

Love, Light & Life—ssw

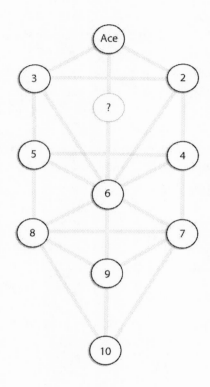

ARI — TREE OF LIFE

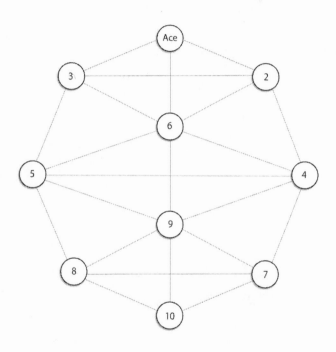

GRA — TREE OF LIFE (RESTORED)

The Spots & Royals

Ace of Wands

We begin with Fire, all the Fire that ever was or ever will be—continually arriving. I fear this Fire, am in awe of it, in need of it, drawn inexplicably to it. As primary outpouring, I am made of this Fire, and am made by it.

All things have a beginning, except That from which all things begin. As the morning sun crowns over the lake, this then the first of my 40 days, my descent and subsequent return.

Here, the Spirit of Will striving for manifestation; here, opportunity and potential wanting to be put to use. Pure desire, pure passion, urge, vitality. In restless awakening the universe trembles at the voice of the One.

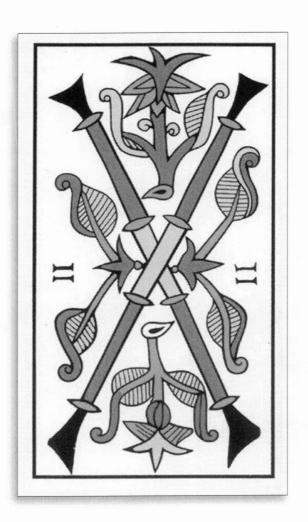

TWO OF WANDS

Initial spark set in motion as energy and force now move forward. For an instant: two, but also sovereign in its pristine wisdom, this first division, sacerdotal polarity. From here: Command and Dominion. I can say, I am myself, as I survey the edge of all that will become.

Centered between oscillating flames of free fall and desire, I'm eager to act. Fully charged and integrated I anticipate this grand adventure.

THREE OF WANDS

*B*ody, Intellect, Spirit—I assign some names to the trinity. But what is space and time to the Will Force? What then is dimension, and how shall I proceed from here on out? My strength is established in this realm. I will call this Virtue.

At this juncture there is no compromise, which is to say there is no turning back. Honesty prevails. We take this chance in unknown worlds, act with integrity. The center remains.

Four of Wands

The law of power, and the power of law—it is Love that desires completion. These flames emerging into being have come together, move in uncharted direction. This is my new home, my haven, my momentary harvest and spiritual success.

Cooperation is called forth from Mercy. The foundation of 4 is holistic. I feel the current of Will manifesting fully as system and order. I take refuge in this union, structured realm of expansion.

Five of Wands

*O*utburst of energy and surge of creative power seeks avenues for expression. The red 5 receives Light from the Jupiterian 4 and through constriction creates the heat necessary for transformation. This is strife!

You feel the restriction, internal combustion, a volcanic eruption as a consequence of pent-up tensions. With discipline and resolve, we'll call this conflict, Creation.

Six of Wands

Poise and power at the center of the tree, arrived we are revitalized. Like a gyro this Logos, victorious beauty. From here, I can see my home on high, from here the bride somewhere in the great below. I consider my love of her, my philo Sophia.

What I do from here benefits the All. Recognition: but not for myself alone. Another word for the 6 is Harmony, so it's win-win as we carry on. Optimism, like Gratitude, is a power.

Seven of Wands

In the misty realm of the fantastic
I reach for courage, the heart space
I knew before. Fire is also a weapon,
and a weapon a majick tool. Whether
by voice or by wave of hand, I stand my
ground for better or for worse.

There are others floating through,
seven times seven and more. I look these
demons in the eye. Character is forged on
this stone—bravery. Valor.

EIGHT OF WANDS

Redirected by feat of mercurial intelligence, I am quickened, exhilarated. With good communication a difficult situation is turned in a positive direction, the bright and brilliant at my back. Prior victory provides enthusiasm. I am direct—beginning with myself.

Act now, they all say, and they say it as one. Swiftly, I engage the Good.

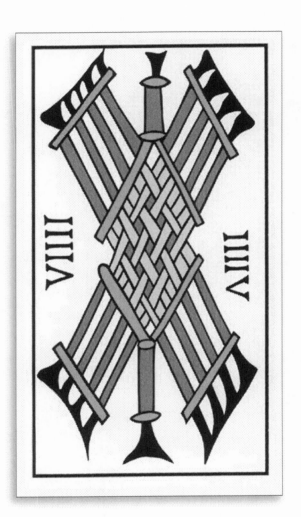

Nine of Wands

If you've come this way, it is not without wound. But here we are renewed, health regained. Through a break in the forest we see the rugged pass and snowy peak behind us, the verdant valley down below. The potency of moon and sun together, of wakefulness within and without, has made us strong.

Resources and spiritual reserves; fires of the vital soul. Alignment!

Ten of Wands

In the rush of my arrival I may have overstepped my bounds. Fire yes, but in whose hand, and where the hidden flame? I see that in this world anything can become too much, brilliance become burnout. With power comes awesome responsibility. To lead is to serve.

Service and duty pale without Soul, become obligation, a burden on the helper, and the helped. Here I release fiery pride and self-oppression, cool my brow with the salve of kindness, reclaim my determined heart.

KNAVE OF WANDS

Restless and pioneering, this young one appears fearless. But courage, like other powers, is a coat s/he will wear until it fits. With a laboratory or box of paints the clean up could be extensive. Mastery here is of spontaneous expression and liberation, an inside job. The innocent soul in its beauty.

There is a recollection that there is no self, save as reflection of the Self, but it dims in the ways of the world. Stay close to the teacher, inner and outer, lest you set all the broom and buckets dancing at once.

F·P·LE·TRENGE·
CHEVALIER·DEBASTON

KNIGHT OF WANDS

*A*s the Air of Fire, the Knight learns to wield outer self confidence, to bring all that creativity into the world—without hurting anyone—and to master inspiration. His element of air gives reason to the underlying Will Force.

Swift and strong, he is a messenger (link) between the spiritual roots of primal fire and our upraised consciousness. Carefree, yes, but like all Knights, he is on a mission. In service to the good Queen, all is well.

REINE · DE · BASTON ·

QUEEN OF WANDS

Her deep water is a lens giving vision to fire. She is a Seer, and her mastery is of Self knowledge. Her inner sight brings feelings to the aggressiveness of fire, and assists the personality in awakening to the deepest essence of who we are.

As supernal aspect of the subconscious, she takes the Sacred Fire and prepares circumstances in the world for execution. You may trust her maturity—she has earned it by sorrow, and by trial.

ROY · DE · BASTONS · ∴

KING OF WANDS

*A*ctive, generous and fierce, he is the Fire of Fire. As a leader/servant he is available to others. All obstacles are burned out the way in his presence. The King mobilizes energy to actualize outward vision.

The Will Force, or desire, is also sexuality, life thrusting forward into the dark recesses of mystery. He is therefore fulfiller, that force within us all that seeks expression of brilliance and plenty.

Ace of Cups

S ea of Love, Oh boundless sea of Love. We say of water that it is fluid, sublime, ever seeking itself. We say that She is the all-encompassing maternal force, the dove as symbol of Venus, as Great Mother.

Source of the soul, I long for union, merging, devotion. Your cup as chalice of my invisible church is container and substance, temple and spirit, form and consciousness.

What flows here, flows eternal, brings compassion to this fiery journey.

Two of Cups

We are parted that we might meet again, this supernal plan of reintegration. To recognize the One everything must first become *other*. Our initial word then is Reflection. Love is our sanctum, and by ones and twos and tribes and galaxy clusters, we include one another until the circle has no circumference.

We hold this precious water between us, our mutual love of Nature, but not all is received in silent ecstasy or hot sex. Relationship is also a demanding work. She blesses each one of us in our various endeavors.

THREE OF CUPS

Conception is fulfillment and this exchange must overflow. Spirit gives form to seeds within, as positive feelings seek to be shared with others. One plus one makes three, and so in the world of conception we have begun.

Love is communal, friends abound: houseplants, spiders, small birds, quirky neighbors, big cats, a lover's love, the wind, a certain star. All is celebration of new life and abundance.

Four of Cups

*A*wellspring of vital life force breaks the surface, flows visible and viable from its subterranean union. This is a luxury of emotion, a brief happiness. Even on the desert, or especially on the desert, an oasis such as this will whisper its location.

All is in balance, and the capacity to comfort others accompanies this wonder. Yearning and devotion are one and the same. Here we may drink our fill, but no more than is needed.

Five of Cups

S everity too must have its way, lest intoxication keep us from our task. Going deeper now, I find the world of feeling both fills and breaks my heart. Emancipation has caused separation.

Disappointed and disillusioned, you feel alone as you face fears of abandonment. A patient and gentle approach is indicated. From here on out grief will accompany you, but as a trustworthy friend.

SIX OF CUPS

Solar radiance (your friend the Sun) penetrates deep into the dark core of psychic mystery. Harmony and Beauty prevail in matters of the heart. The reciprocity of giving and receiving brings renewal, Innocence.

Letting go of disappointment is rewarded as once again the Light shines from inside out. At this station, Truth is revealed.

SEVEN OF CUPS

Her love, boundless in the realm of imagination, has created emotional overextension. I feel *strange*. Phantasmagoria coming and going, illusion, self-deception—this hall of watery mirrors. "Yoda, how do I choose?"

Patterns of over indulgence have depleted vital energies, veiled the Truth. You must mobilize vision and imagination in service to Spirit. Direct the Force.

Eight of Cups

I arrive exhausted, in need of reason and structure. Boundaries! And I admit that some soils need either more tending or to be left well enough alone to their sparse and wild natures. In either case—action, not stagnation.

Life proceeds from a thought; it is here that limits are set, the compass pointed. Perhaps I'll let the blackberries range on the rocky slopes as they prefer. Acceptance is also transformation.

NINE OF CUPS

Water of faith, water of love, this is Blessedness. The sensual wellspring of happiness has found its perennial source, takes pleasure in delivering. Goodwill cycles as river, ocean, cloud and rain, and renews all aspects of human life.

This is emotional breakthrough, integration, the soul at peace. At last, a trust in Life.

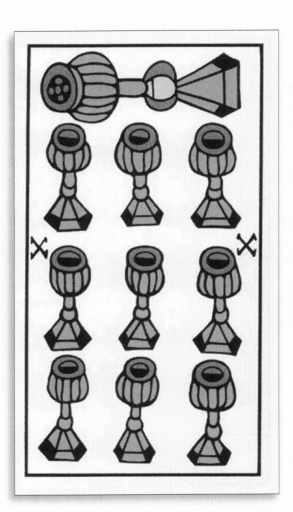

TEN OF CUPS

River of Love flowing from the One. Now I understand the "fire of water," its holy radiance. Satisfaction from deep within finds outward expression as passion and vitality. I feel this is a successful way of living.

And now I know that contentment cannot be contained, and humility more than ever must be a trusted guide. To consent to the opened heart and let Love flow to others is the Way of the Current, but crusading is an unnecessary posture.

VALET·DE·COVPES·

KNAVE OF CUPS

*A*s a dreamer, the Knave will master emotional objectivity. The task—to bring the groundedness of earth to the watery realm of the imagination. Listen, as s/he brings messages from the unconscious, and lends substance to higher ideals. The scarf indicates a quest for the Madonna.

In learning to love and be loved, one must have a conviction to not abandon one's self, to trust rather than control. On our way to being a Queen or King we respond to intuition, are keen to universal patterns of the Over Soul, always seeking Conscious Harmony.

F·P·LE·TRENGE·X
CHEVALIER·DE·COVPE

KNIGHT OF CUPS

*D*rawn to love and/or pursuit of inner life, the Knight may be devoted to a partner, or involved with dreams and the romance of wisdom. Oh, Sufi heart, troubadour of truth, the world is your soul mate.

Clear thinking is a medium for expressing the depths of the soul. And in this awakening, a responsibility to humanity. He is a bridge between intuition and reason.

REINE·DECOVPES ◆

QUEEN OF CUPS

Psychically in tune with Mystery, she is the female presence of the Divine within us. As Listener and clairaudient, she is relational with the ability to give deep nurturing. Mastery of emotional integrity.

Selflessness comes from higher expressions of the soul, the chalice is dwelling place of Sacred Love. House of all the veiled mysteries which dwell in shadow, yet flow forth cohesively. Isn't she beautiful?

· ROY · DE · COVPES ·

KING OF CUPS

It's loyalty and commitment at this stage of development, a king who can manifest harmonious situations. This is love beyond ego and vanity. Graceful, poetic, diplomatic—outer love.

And who better than one who has come through their own dark night of the soul to give emotional support, positively express the Life-Will. At home with the unconscious, receptivity leads naturally to creative inspiration. Fire of Water.

Ace of Swords

I think, he said, therefore... and then there was light, and all followed accordingly. What is formed is formed here first; from every center each new instant is that primal thought. Behold, the Diamond Mind.

Perception, clarity, objectivity— I have become aware my awareness. Mindfulness is not a chill out, but the graceful undoing of that which is simply not for me.

Without responsibility ideas can be dynamic but erratic, justice or punishment. Beware the tendency to believe the next thing you think. The palm leaf of suffering or the olive branch of peace—in your hand the sword of discernment. Invoke what you will.

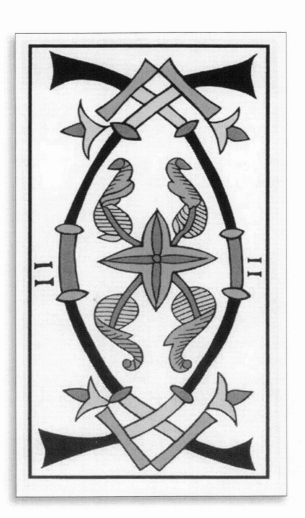

Two of Swords

This is thinking that polarizes the world in order to comprehend it, a counter balance through the finding of knowledge. Our two interwoven strands of DNA insure it. Two eyes focused forward give reason, meaning and depth to creation. Perception is mirror.

Now, an appreciation for unity, for powers reconciled, for Peace restored. Thriving, more than ever, requires renunciation, shutting out distractions. Therefore, Inner focus. Contemplation.

THREE OF SWORDS

What is this universal sorrow? Expelled from heaven or birthed into the world, we experience constriction of the womb, gravity, time, all the lessons of Saturnian limitation. From this perception of dejection has come helplessness and grief.

This storm has ultimately come from within—a memory of the beginning of time. Recommitted to work in the world, I challenge this distrustful outlook, cast off old spells. This adjustment is the destruction of the obsolete rising from my sacred flaming heart.

Four of Swords

Life solves problems. That's what it does. The sublime 2 now doubled as the perfect 4 has found stability, recovery, recuperation. A time for cleansing and integration. This is the Hermit's repose.

Retreat to the Temple of your Heart. Keep still. Life, which seeks in every moment to transcend itself, is busy forming heretofore-unseen worlds. Establish a truce, a time for Incubation. Revel in the mind washed clean.

FIVE OF SWORDS

The rose of Venus has been wounded. Fear has stepped into the picture, and now others are involved. The group is not of one mind— nor need it be. They say wars are fought over resources, but I say it's all identity, ideology, a thought that thinks there is room only for itself.

So this is defeat, or the fear of it. Rejoice in the discovery of these old ideas that no longer work. Discord becomes opportunity. Senseless fighting—What in the world was I thinking? Room for everything is real power!

SIX OF SWORDS

*A*nd yes, as she said, the Self continuously transcends itself. The rose of recognition has bloomed within our knowing. With Beauty as principle, science is established in its proper role and function. This is Thinking with Heart.

Restored to sanity, the soul presses through another veil, flowers in the mind-body-personality as spiritual technology. Feed the Rose! We'll need this intelligence, this moment of harmonious objectivity, in the days to come, in the stages of evolution ahead.

SEVEN OF SWORDS

Suddenly I'm despondent and discouraged, the weight of my emotions has distorted the single sword. I have imagined unreasonable fears. Oh, these undifferentiated feelings, these "crows of dispersion."

Everywhere this watery vacillation. I must my master doubt, take a stand against self-sabotage. Ambiguity has called for commitment—advance or withdrawal, action or rest. I follow only this thread of Truth, the noble song of myself.

Eight of Swords

Too much feeling, now too much thinking; I am tossed from one coast to another. The signal is diffused—I'm picking up truckers on the radio, intergalactic pirates, bugs in the tree.

Intellect here is a mighty force, a necessary tool and reckoning for those whose destiny lay beyond. Arrived at another initiation, I am hoodwinked, forced to retreat, to seek answers within.

The power of 8 reiterates itself on a higher octave. With focused ceremony, what was interference becomes the clear broadcast of unified mind. I admit now that I need the assistance of those who have gone before.

NINE OF SWORDS

A nightmare has revealed the dream for what it is. I had believed too many of the world's ideas. I was walking and talking in my sleep. I will embrace the first child I see, and taking them in my arms I will shield them from zombies, from further self-cruelty.

You are loved, I will say, you are loved without merit and beyond measure. This is a moment of awakening, the dark moon giving way to the sun, the work of fire, water and air just before dawn. A strike of beneficent lightning, a visitation of cosmic concern.

Ten of Swords

Not by happenstance, all those previous stages have led to this, this moment of necessary ruin. But also Release, Reversal, and Renewal. No wonder I found it hard to vote; I always saw all the possibilities within a thing; polarities were just a range of infinitude. And I wondered if I might be going insane.

Finally relieved of small thoughts, I direct my will toward the recognition and achievement of Good. This is an end for which I've been searching, therefore— a Promise.

· VALET · DEPEES ·

Knave of Swords

The Earth of Air, s/he is learning to master practical thinking, to be keen but cautious with good emotional boundaries. As mood fighter the Knave applies ideas in tangible and productive ways.

An initiator and link between the psyche and soma. S/he considers the power of reason, learns to use the sword to cut through the outer veils of psychological patterns of causation. Down to earth considerations.

F · P · LE · TRENGE :::
CHEVALIER · DESPEIS

KNIGHT OF SWORDS

Quick principled, he charges directly into the storm, totally focused. Analytical and impersonal, he needs a frame of reference on which to base personal truths. He will need to master creative and intuitive thinking.

The inspired mind which does not want to be limited. Outlaw protector. The Knight slays the ferries of egoic thought that pull his chariot off course.

· REINE · DESPEIES

QUEEN OF SWORDS

Capable and quick, she is a professional, a counselor, a consultant. Perceptive of pattern more than particulars, she reflects the bigger picture.

The Queen cuts through her own masks, roles and defenses in service to Truth. Ego slayer and liberator of mind, her commitment gives her purpose. Sometimes sorrowful and alone, there is a cost to efficient objectivity.

· ROY·DESPEE ·

KING OF SWORDS

Intellectual prowess without much emotion, he constantly considers consequences. This is the highly evolved rational intellect. Lecturer and teacher, he is fierce and skillful. Communicator!

His maturity will help him master passionate thinking and intentionality, lest his super developed reason cut him off from Higher Will.

Ace of Coins

*A*nd now the world for which we have been preparing... for which we have *been prepared.* Within this eternal bursting—nature, sanctuary, fruition, abundance, the invisible made visible. This is the body of the Divine, our body the cosmos.

If you think this majick union is a handful of dirt, you're right of course, but you'll never again see so-called matter the same. The mundane is the culmination of all intelligences. I own nothing here, but use whatever I desire. As nucleus and seed, the One is self-contained.

TWO OF COINS

*A*bove ground, one delicate leaf, then another. Alternation of warmth and rain, light and night. I can no longer deny the Harmony here. It's change that brings real stability, transformation driven by rhythm, the cosmic swaying and breathing of Her.

I walk in beauty and bloom into being before my very eyes. I exist in a myriad of opposites—this is not dualism!

Learning the secret of equilibration, I reach out and touch the expression of wisdom at work in the world.

Three of Coins

Will is converted by effort into results, but it's not so much the product as the work. There is satisfaction in the doing. I am artist, architect and magi. But who laid the corner stone? Whose central idea brings all this into being?

Discipline and cooperation are mastery, vigilance its own bliss. The crystallization of force into form is Creative Work. This is a trinity you can wrap your body around, participate in with heart and hands.

Four of Coins

A place for everything, and everything in its place—now I get it. All the elements contribute to the whole. Integrity is being the same through and through. I am crossed within this cube of space, pinned to the ground, then lifted up.

His outgoing goodness gives new dimension to law and order. I couldn't see it when asking the wrong questions. They told me that hoarding was practical, but knew little of it. Manifestation, as it turns out, is absolutely brilliant!

FIVE OF COINS

This pentagram is upside down, unstable in its reversal. Materialism, the prioritizing of matter over spirit, creates more suffering. In that dream, there is never enough—of anything. Just unnecessary pessimism and brooding. Mars all by himself.

Moderation, however, has nothing to do with unworthiness. Some souls explore it even further... ascetic lifestyles and renunciation are for the contemplative warrior who knows, or will soon find out, that she already possesses everything.

Six of Coins

*A*s within, so without. My appreciation of the world is an inside job. Gratitude and generosity beget one another. The law of attraction (which is no joke) lets me know what remains in my way.

I thought I would wait until I had enough, you know, *some extra*, and then start giving. She calls this postponing enlightenment. Refusing to receive stops the flow just as much as refusing to give—same thing. This 6 is an emanation of True Prosperity.

Seven of Coins

Writers block, they call it, but everyone knows what I'm talking about. The artist sitting on the floor in their studio, head in hands, telephone ringing. Hesitation, resignation, life on pause. Or maybe it's necessary deliberation.

What is forming in the imaginal is working in its own realm. Patience, reflection and humility are indicated for Victory. Deal with fears, not with what the world calls "failure." Mystery moves us along at her own pace, slower or faster, depending upon rhythms beyond our understanding.

EIGHT OF COINS

The structure of this station facilitates the budding of possibilities. The Earth is wise and sure-footed. Here we protect and nourish this unfoldment as it flowers on a higher plane. After all, it is the majick 8 manifesting in the final world.

Prudence then, like the seasons, is built on pattern and repetition. Keep doing the good thing. Since Mercury is involved, we'll call this Applied Knowledge—a little forethought, a little skill, some self-discipline.

NINE OF COINS

Gain has come from giving, and now it is real-ized. The Moon makes it so. It's okay to feel satisfied with our increase and outcome. Besides, as conduit for the Divine, this growth and fulfillment doesn't exactly belong to us. This is the Shekinah here on Earth.

As we gather this season's Harvest we notice some room for improvement, but that doesn't diminish our Joy. Engage deeply. Delight in existence.

Ten of Coins

Wealth has taken on new meaning and dimension, this our final ceremony and initiation. The Pure Will of the Divine has been drawn down into manifestation, brought full circle into our heaven. Now I turn with her to head for home, begin again.

As the sun slips over the desert edge, my barque lifts into a canopy of stars, the unfathomable beyond. It has only been a single sojourn, yet, it feels like the Completion of a Great Work.

Knave of Coins

M astery of creativity and birth of new forms. Learning inner security, s/he is kind, generous, diligent and preserving. Aesthetic appreciation and creative motherhood. S/he obeys the earthly, ancient passion to create.

That desire and principle which is "...done on earth as in heaven." All is pregnant with meaning, and here, Life and Will are one.

F · P · LE✕TRENGE
CHEVALIER · DE · DENIER

KNIGHT OF COINS

*B*uilder, but also protector, of earthly forms. Strong and reliable, here is an architect and designer. Investor, entrepreneur.

This is the power of reason applied to practical things. Link between thought and event, he stands as the agency of equilibration between the light and dark aspects of manifestation.

· REINE · DEDENIER ·

QUEEN OF COINS

S he builds up, tears down, is Gaia. She sees herself as caretaker of her possessions—rather than owner, possesses inner security. As Mother Earth she brings creative action to fruition. Provider!

The Queen of Coins perceives patterns of cyclicity, change and movement. She contemplates the mysteries of earth, and maintains her deep connection with the spiritual through it.

· ROY · DE · DENIES ·

King of Coins

Producer and master of natural resources, he cultivates and integrates land, people and ideas. This is abundance and prosperity manifest through supernal wisdom. Responsible husbandry.

One with every detail of creation; seed-power of earth. Lord of the wild and fertile lands, he is the good king, Steward, environmentalist supreme.

2

THE HIGH CARDS

LE·FOL·

Fool

Stumbling bum or sacred clown, a babe blinking new eyes in an unknown world. Innocence with impulse. Limitless potential of all beginnings. Unconditional Life-power awaits activation. A smile, rather than a frown.

In sight: this is the eye. In speech: the open mouth. Too foolish to be intimidated by intelligence or position, s/he steps out on the invisible bridge. As mirror image of all the High Cards, the Fool accompanies every process, is then a Hidden Force.

MAGICIAN

My first act of will—a wish to be in the world. It worked! Tehuti/Hermes is tongue with heart, directing vibration through speech, pointing a stick, the alchemist's resolve to take on the Great Work.

He invokes and manifests sequence. Through keen intention the Magician transforms consciousness.

Do not acquire power, direct it, by effortless will, effortless concentration.

PRIESTESS

On some Tarots those are the horns of the Sacred Mother cow, none other than the Sun rising between them. I create the veils I wear, hold within me all the principles—polarity, rhythm, cause and effect, vibration, gender, all memory and Akashic Record, the Book of Life.

As Cosmic Mind-stuff, you call me collective unconscious, but also am I the Pure Receptive. My "Listening" is sufficient unto itself. Without Mind, the Magician has nowhere in which to sing his thoughts. Spontaneous meditation.

Empress

*A*s Queen of Earth—temporal ruler. As doorway—The Gate of Heaven. All that manifests passes through Her (coming *and* going). Fertile Mother, Venus and devotion. She is also the subconscious, immaculate yet fertile.

All things having to do with reproduction, organization, formation, and arrangement, what happens here in the world. Thoughts begin to take form as definite mental images, therefore—Creative Imagination.

EMPEROR

Through the agency of the Empress, also a ruler. Universal power of realization. Radiant and expansive mental energies, the vision and insight required to oversee and supervise construction of the world—but not a power for humankind to abuse.

Evolving from myth to Reason! Analytic by Nature, the Emperor seeks the causal foundation of phenomena. Highly motivated and fully disciplined, he seeks to understand the needs of environment, community, clan and family.

HIEROPHANT

Perception of the power and presence of the Inner Voice. This is the teacher, the teaching, your holy guardian angel. Instructor to the "Children of the Art." Intuition!

As with the circulation of blood and breath, prayer rises and descends, renews and cleanses. These are the very angels you sent, a good reason for obedience. Receive this benediction.

LOVERS

A painful awareness of separation spawns immediate desire to unite. The Path presents itself. Narrow is the way, noble your intention. Urge and method, imagination and discrimination, this is the sacred marriage that will shatter the bonds of the material world.

Intimate relationship within the Self. Integration, but not necessarily agreement, between the lower and higher, all administered by an Arch Angel. Sub-conscious, self-conscious, super-conscious—another way to view the trinity.

CHARIOT

The inner has taken form, the enclosure of the personality is poised for engagement. This is the hero as vehicle. A stillness in motion. Triumph.

Instinct, passion and reason work together, overcoming obstacles of fear and addictive patterns, learning to relate positively to others. Exploration, valor and acceptance, yes, but remember the goal—transformation. Onward.

JUSTICE

The Truth will prevail. No need to "reform" the world. Instead come into accord, conform to the "Immovable Order of Things." As Karmic Law, she is the Balance between all the cosmic forces.

The uninitiated carry on about "chaos" without true understanding, but friend—this IS order. Our task then is to ask what is right, what is righteous.

The cord to parents has been cut, it is I who must evaluate myself, prune and adjust. Not what others think of me, but what I think of myself, how I measure up. Forgiveness is inherent in the cosmic design. This is Art in service to Nature, *never punishment.*

Hermit

*A*ll our searching through books, maps and mystic drawings, through chants, circles and fire-lit dramas, is finally set aside as scaffolding and reflection. Inward looking, yet detached, this is not isolation.

Monastic tradition began in the desert, a place that is clean, a life that is chosen. Mastery of contemplation and yoga, the sacred arts.

The Hermit now holds his own light, just enough to illumine the immediate path. A single beam from this lantern will become the Lightning Strike, then the eight-pointed Star.

Wheel

The Whirling Wholeness and the teaching of return. The karmic wheel rotates through polarities— through growth and decay followed by birth. In the center, I do nothing! At the edge, poverty and wealth. I wait for the moment to act, seize the day.

Course of an afternoon, course of a year, course of a cosmos—I step back from destiny and fortune, take another look. I observe the cyclic patterns of my life at play, catch more than a glimpse of immortality. Who continues?

Strength

Not armored, but barefoot, she knows that Nature is her ally. Stage by stage we have been built, one dynamic step becoming the platform of the next. But no need to rebuke instinct.

Wild Desire is the forging of Life into form, the feet upon which we run, the howling of our ancestry toward the stars. Perhaps it is the younger, rational mind that must be tamed.

Reaching deeper into the core, I hold in my hand the molten heart of earth, the animal, the intellect, the soaring song of God's wish for me. This is Power.

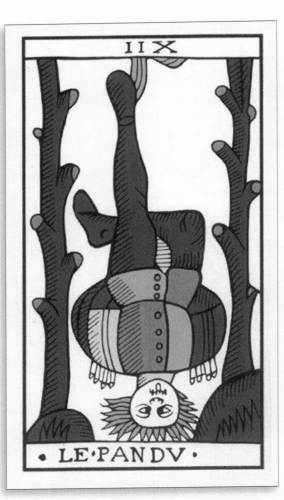

Hanged One

Do not think me asleep, nor tortured as a traitor. I am self-suspended, dreaming lucidly with my head pointed toward the volcano. Sacrificed by my own volition, I refuse to participate in unenlightened activities. I investigate the interior of the Earth.

I am no longer enamored with personality, and so I don't swing back and forth against the walls of it. My dependency, as you can see, is on something higher.

Death

There are many "secrets" of the Great Work. And this generative power and ongoing liberation is certainly one. Death is a dissolution and transformation of Substance, but never an ultimate end. Without this loving Promise, all would be lifeless matter, a cruel hoax.

Here is the teaching about True Imagination, about the death of lies (even the spiritual and recent ones). Nothing escapes this dismantling. Any questions about supremacy?

TEMPERANCE

We are infused by holy light, tempered, tested, made anew. We are the stone start to finish; we are none of these. All forms are returned to Source for transmutation. I observe my thoughts, ideas that wear thin while others emerge clear, more suited for the journey.

The androgynous angel is Higher Self, water pourer, inner alchemist. The middle road is goal and result. Mediation, moderation, composure. Fire in one hand, ice in the other, the paths are many as the Life Force reconciles opposites within us—each according to our own natural design.

DEVIL

The Devil says, "What sensation reports is all there is." But could She be God misunderstood by the wicked, another gatekeeper on the return flight? Our apparent separateness is the delight of the Divine. Individuality (*ego perception*) is evidently inherent in the grand scheme.

As odd friend and advocate this one shows us the bonds of false attachment, offers release. Perhaps "evil" then is our own creation, a momentary misconception. Whoever said that Nature was an enemy to be conquered must have thought themselves small and afraid. But here is emancipation!

TOWER

This is my longing striking in both directions, awakening of aroused attention. Some feel it first at the base of the spine, others as a house on fire that takes their head off. This is a reckoning! When it's time to fly, all hell breaks loose. Nothing false survives the House of God.

Behold, the life-breath of every creature, the motion of us all. Energy is released, but no problem is solved until some structure of ignorance is dissolved, some stronghold of error. This is another Gateway of the Soul, the rising of Kundalini, as they say in the East. But alas, our work is still here on the ground.

STAR

I n order of apparent magnitude, now a point of light that I can follow, the first in this clearing of sky and opening of the celestial realm. She is Natural Intelligence, the highest of the feminine principle. Ladder of the Seven Planets, Realm of the Stars, Gateway to Heaven—this glimpse of ascension. Hope!

Oh my Fool, my traveller, what miracles have germinated in darkness! In meditation the Star will regulate and mediate the transfer of spiritual energies—but you must *ask* Her. She offers Vision and Revelation. By chance is that Tehuti in the Tree?

Moon

A final plunge into the dreamtime of shadows—playful, erotic, enticing, mad and malcontent. Swelling and shrinking of tides, the wonder and beauty of a silent, reflected light. Gentle but ill-defined she beckons us to look beyond the veil. Still in the grip of matter, Art must perfect the wild body given by Nature. Sleep, therefore, Repair.

Not fully formed, you must molt again. Do not hate the body if you wish to move on. Here again is the pool of Mind-stuff where the initiate learns to move with the expansion and contraction of conscious states. The world is organized here—you are being shown the kitchen.

SUN

In every culture, a myth of the Twins, a story of death and rebirth, of re-unification. This is a pilgrimage to the Self, conscious identification with the One, a new realization of personality and That which generates it.

If the Star is prophetic, the Moon transformative, the Sun then is Self-aware. This light cannot be seen with the body, though its bright interior bathes all within your gaze, radiates from the inside out. So in a mysterious way, it's no longer your affair.

ANGEL

These coffins are made of matter, time and space in 3 dimensions, dreams that held up the wall, a mass hallucination, the Matrix. Pick up your beds and walk. This is the end of the delusion of separateness.

The marriage now consummated, the ordeal with the Devil done, the twins re-integrated. Everybody rise, the hoax is over. Liberation. Joy of Release!

WORLD

Having dipped into the bowl, realized the What of it, come full circle home, I find myself here and here again. A cycle so to speak, a completion without end. Balance of Body, Soul & Mind; knowledge, but not about details—this is Divine Gnosis.

Active participation in the cosmic government now charged with full responsibility for execution of its laws.

As administrator I act with and for The All as I design worlds to come. Co-creator, and babe once again... the Great Work has just begun.

LE·FOL·

FOOL

Filled and emptied again, I am the hands and eyes of Her, the chalice and star—nobody in particular. What I'm looking for is what I'm looking with. And you may make of This what you will.

Always moving forward, even when falling down, stillness at the speed of Light, eternal youth. Others may have the glory of knowing, but it is Life Itself that is noble.

All is in the journey, all in the going. You could say, then, that I am the Way of the Current.

Made in the USA
Charleston, SC
08 January 2015